Degus as Pets

A Complete Degu Care Guide

The Must Have Guide for Anyone
Passionate about Owning a Degu,
Includes Health, Diet, Housing and
Lots More…

By Susan Moore

Foreword

How did the degu evolve? Well, it depends on what group of scientists you ask. One bunch will tell you that about 55 million years ago, some ancestor of all the existing South American rodents came wandering down from North America.

Another, equally "certain" theory suggests an African animal crossed over the Atlantic Ocean at a time when the continents were closer together. These intrepid "explorers" may even have been riding "rafts" made of clumped up twigs.

For our purposes, however, we can jump forward to the 1960s when degus were first brought to both the United States and Great Britain. The first twenty imported adults went to the Massachusetts Institute of Technology for research purposes.

The descendants of those degus had an easier time of it, becoming residents at the National Zoo. Like most cute, furry little creatures, the degu ultimately attracted the attention of enthusiasts as a companion animal.

When you first see a degu you have a sense that you're looking at some sort of rodent, but a degu is more like a squirrel than a rat. In fact, degus are sometimes called Chilean squirrels – or brush-tailed rats or trumpet rats.

Foreword

There are other members of the genus *Octodon*, but the little creature that has won the hearts of enthusiasts is specifically *Octodon degus*.

Unlike the vast majority of rodents, this happy little fellow is wide awake during the day, has been to known to live as long as 13 years in captivity, has a bushy tail, and fastidious personal habits.

After an initial period of making your acquaintance, degus enjoy giving and receiving attention. Like chinchillas, they bathe in dust to keep their coats clean and healthy, which is arguably one of the cutest things they do.

Scientists studying brain function have a keen interest in this species. When young degus are taken away from their mothers they exhibit severe separation anxiety and later develop behavioral problems that are identical to ADHD in humans.

As they age, degus exhibit neural markers that are very similar to those seen in Alzheimer's patients, a condition never before detected in a wild rodent.

Intelligent, with a proven ability to solve problems, degus make intriguing pets with a fairly low maintenance profile.

In behavioral studies, the beguiling little animals have used sticks as rakes to retrieve objects they otherwise could not reach, and have organized items by size.

Foreword

The more you get to know your degu, the more convinced you will be that your pet knows exactly what you're thinking – often before you think it.

They are somewhat prone to diabetes and cataracts, but if housed and fed correctly, degus are hardy, happy companions. Although not as easy to acquire as other pet rodents, degus are growing rapidly in popularity as companion animals.

Exclusive Free Offer

Join other Degu lovers and owners in our unique **FREE** club – Exclusive to owners of this book.

See page 27 on how to join easily in seconds (and free)

Receive discounts on Degu supplies like food and housing. Connect with others members to share knowledge and experience, ask questions. The best place for lovers of these amazing animals.

Table of Contents

Table of Contents

Table of Contents

Table of Contents

Table of Contents

Chapter 1 – Introduction to the Degu

If you've never heard of a degu, you're not alone. In the wild, you will only find this tiny rodent in the Andes

Mountains in Chile, and then only on the western slopes.

Their native concentrations are dense, sometimes numbering as many as 100 degus per acre. Individual groups or "colonies" number 8-10 members.

Degus can live at elevations as high as 3,937 feet (1,200 meters), but unlike their close relative the chinchilla, they don't thrive at higher altitudes.

Chapter 1 – Introduction to the Degu

In recent years, the degu has emerged as a popular pet in North America and Europe. They adapt well to life as companion animals, and have a way of charming people on first sight, with their big, black eyes, and intelligent, perky ears.

Specific Environmental Adaptations

The degu's preferred environment is in semi-arid, warm areas closer to sea level. Both their anatomy and their life habits are geared toward cooling and water conservation in the cells of the body.

Use of Burrows

They dig burrows interconnected with tunnels to hide from predators, and as a cool refuge during the heat of the day. These same spaces serve as sleeping chambers, food storage bins, and rearing quarters for their young (called pups.)

Degus do not, however, live entirely in their burrows. A significant part of each day is spent "up top" foraging for food, making them "semifossorial" animals.

Diurnal Activity

Degus are diurnal, meaning they are most active during the day. There are, however, seasonal variations in their levels of activity. In the summer, they are only above ground in the morning and evening.

Blood flow in the ears lowers their body temperature since these little animals don't sweat. Additionally, specialized cells in the nasal passages limit water loss while breathing.

Their primary dietary components are native herbs and grasses that are highly fibrous and tough. Like all rodents, degus' teeth grow throughout their lives as compensation for the abrasive nature of their food source.

Social Groups

Highly social by nature, degus live in groups comprised on average of 1 or 2 males and as many as 6 females. It's also common to see some smaller all-male groups of confirmed bachelors!

Social groups are a further adaptation to provide protection from native predators like buzzards and foxes. Group members stand watch by turns while other degus are digging burrows or finding food.

Physical Characteristics

At birth, a degu weighs only half an ounce (14 grams). By the time they reach their full adult size, degus weigh 6-10.5 ounces (170-300 grams) and measure 5-8 inches (12-20 cm) plus an added 5 inches (12 cm) for their generous tails.

Lifespan in Captivity

Your pet degu should live 6-8 years on average, which is about three times longer than pet rats and roughly five times longer than hamsters.

It is worth noting that degus are so affectionate and have such outstanding dispositions owners report great difficulty when the inevitable happens and their pet dies.

Saying good-bye is the hardest part of having any companion animal, but most people erroneously assume that it's easier to let some kinds of pets go than others. This is certainly not the case with a degu.

Bodily Conformation

In build, the degu is a robust, solid little creature. Nature designed these squirrel-like rodents to be compact and agile. When they think danger is afoot, degus slip easily into the most improbable spaces.

The front legs and paws are much smaller than those in the back. Degus use their forepaws to hold food and to manipulate objects in their environment.

Legs and Feet

The back legs, though larger in proportion, still seem tiny and fragile to the human eye. In reality, the hind limbs are deceptively powerful.

The pads of all four feet resemble those of a dog or cat and are rough in texture. This fatty tissue protects the feet and also helps the degu establish traction. Each foot has five toes, but only four are well developed.

Degus climb gracefully and well, run very quickly, and are capable of leaping several feet. Catching a pet degu on the loose is no easy matter.

Tail

A degu's tail is extremely fragile and will come right off the animal's body with very little force required to accomplish the severance. This is called "de-gloving."

You certainly never want to grab a degu by the tail or you'll be left holding the appendage in your hand.

The degu reacts to this situation with great practicality, biting the remaining piece down to a stump once it has dried. The wound will heal quickly, but the tail will not grow back.

Degus use their tails for visual displays in communication and also beat them against the floor to send audible signals.

Subtle Coloration

The soft body fur of the degu is gray to brown in tone, with just a hint of yellow in certain lights. Over the eyes, however, the pale yellow is distinct, and emphasizes the little creature's alert expression.

The body color is not a constant solid, but is "agouti," meaning there are shaded bands on each hair. The result is superb camouflage against sandy soils.

It's not unusual to see a lighter band or collar around the neck, with creamy yellow fur on the belly. The feet are either gray or white.

Short, dark brown bristles cover the tail, growing longer toward the tip where they form a long tuft.

There have been some attempts in captivity to genetically engineer color variations in blue, champagne, white, and patched tones. These efforts have not resulted in healthy individuals, however.

Once or twice a year a degu will molt completely. Typically this happens in the spring when the animal needs to get rid of its heavier winter coat for the coming warm months.

Well-Developed Senses

In partnership, all of a degu's keenly developed senses render the little animal as functionally alert as it appears. This bright demeanor is part of the degu's considerable appeal. Owners routinely mention their pet's great awareness of everything going on in the room.

When a degu sits up on its hind legs, whiskers twitching inquisitively, eyes darting about curiously, he's almost irresistible.

The animal's sensory abilities are also vital to its survival as a prey animal, efficiently alerting it to the presence of predators and triggering the degu's "fight or flight" response.

Given the degu's size, however, the typical response is flight – straight down into its burrow!

Vision

Degus use their excellent daytime vision to spot predators, but also as a means of communication. Their perception of the world truly is colored – in green!

Unlike humans, they can also perceive UV light. They do not, however, have good vision in low light.

Hearing

A degu's acute hearing is vital to its survival. Typically the ears are described as "kidney shaped" and are one of the degu's most distinctive features. Fine hair covers the ears but coarser guard hairs are found at the opening to the ear canal.

In captivity, watching a degu's ears will give you a sense of how the animal is feeling about the ambient temperature. If your pet's ears are up and flushed pink with an infusion of blood, he's hot. If his ears are pale and held down closer to the head, he's cold.

Nose and Whiskers

A degu's hairless nose, flanked by its generous whiskers, is almost constantly in motion reading the scent markings that are an integral part of their social lives. Degus breathe exclusively through their noses.

The whiskers, known as vibrissae, are themselves sensory organs and are especially useful to the degu in judging whether or not its body can fit into any given space.

Determining Gender

In truth, there is very little difference between males and females in either overt appearance or disposition. Establishing gender, however, is not that difficult.

Simply examine the degu's anogenital region at the base of the tail. The safest way to do this, due to the fragile nature of the tail structure, is to tempt your pet to stand up on its hind legs by offering it a treat.

Look for two physical structures, the cone and anus. The cone will be the higher of the two, and is present in both genders. The anus is the second opening closest to the tail.

In a male degu there is a definite gap between the two structures that is roughly equal to the width of your little finger. In females, there is no gap.

You can sex a degu regardless of its age using this method. It even works with pups that are just minutes or hours old. This fact helps enormously in placing babies in new homes.

Degus in the Rodent Family

As rodents, degus share many of the predictable traits common to their kind:

- Four incisor teeth located in upper and lower pairs.
- Teeth that grow throughout their lives.
- Molars used for grinding.

A degu has 20 teeth in total and when the incisors are healthy, they are a startlingly bright orange.

Caviomorphs vs. Myomorphs

Degus are caviomorphs, as are, chinchillas and guinea pigs. Most of the rodents in the word are myomorphs. The principle difference in the two groups is how their young are born.

Myomorphs give birth to helpless offspring that are born naked with their eyes closed. Caviomorphs have young that are born with their eyes open, and look like miniature versions of their parents.

Degus as Pets

Degus are highly agreeable about living in the company of humans. They thoroughly enjoy being held (on their own terms) and will sit still to be petted as long as you'll keep it up, but they aren't needy. They'll just as happily play on their own, and they are truly generous with their affection.

They can, however, be clever little escape artists if you give them even less than half a chance. When a degu gets a long, straight stretch to sprint, he's incredibly fast. Catching a bouncing degu with a head start can be close to impossible.

Male or Female, One or Two?

These two factors have to be discussed in tandem for several reasons. First, degus really are very social and if at

all possible, you should keep more than one.

If you have a lone degu, your little pet will rely on you completely for attention and interaction. Let's face it. You can be a great friend to your degu, but you're not one of his kind. Degus like to have degu buddies!

Obviously, however, you don't want to keep a male and female unless you plan to breed your pets, something I discuss fully later in this book.

The good news is that pairs of either gender get along just fine. There is also no discernible difference in temperament and personality between the genders, so it really doesn't matter which you choose to keep as a pet.

Degus and Other Pets

As rodents, degus are on the "menu" for just about every predator in the world. Cats became domesticated for one purpose – killing rats. Fluffy isn't going to care if the rodent in question is a "designer label" variety or not.

Even the most placid, well-mannered cat is still a cat. Instinct will kick in. If you have a cat in the same house with a degu, make sure the door to your little rodent's cage is secure and can't be pried open by clever feline paws.

In the best of all possible scenarios, you won't give the cat access to the same room in which the degus are kept. Just put yourself in the degus' place. Would you want to be stared at by a would-be predator hour after hour?

Don't count on a dog completely ignoring a degu, especially if you have a terrier breed. Many small dogs were bred to be hunters, and some are, by instinct "ratters."

Bigger dogs might mistake the degu for a chew toy and seriously harm or kill the little animal without really meaning to. The same is true of ferrets and birds, and don't even think about allowing large pet reptiles around these little guys.

If you are sensing a basic line of reasoning, you are correct. Degus and other pets don't mix. To just about every carnivore in the world, your little rodent looks like one thing – lunch.

Degus and Children

Be extremely careful not to let small children handle a degu unattended. There's a significant risk of the small animal being dropped and severely injured, but also of improper handling that may lead to its tail coming off.

Frankly, a degu takes losing his tail remarkably in stride, but this will undoubtedly be traumatizing for the child. It's important that children be taught to handle all animals gently and with respect.

Older children can take a greater role in caring for a degu, but they should understand that loud noises and sudden movement may frighten the little animal. Remember that degus are fast and once they get away, they're hard to catch.

All in all, it's better not to let children take care of degus on their own, and to interact with them only when an adult is there to supervise.

Degus are suitable to be kept as pets in classrooms due to their gregarious nature and low maintenance needs, but the children must not be given unsupervised access to the little animals.

All interaction should be under the teacher's direction and in a contained area. Especially due to the danger of the tail coming off, it's best to keep the door of the cage locked when a degu is kept in a classroom.

Housing Degus with Other Animals

Although degus, chinchillas, and guinea pigs are closely related and have many similarities, don't try to house them together. The same caution holds for rabbits.

This is not so much a matter of the animals not getting along. Each species has distinct dietary needs, and mixing the foods can be quite dangerous.

Rabbit pellets, for instance, should never be given to degus. (See the section on diet and nutrition for more information.)

You also have to consider the animal's habits. Degus are diurnal. They're up and about all day ready for their next adventure.

Chinchillas are nocturnal, happily watching TV at 3 in the morning. (That's not a joke. Many "chin" owners leave the TV or stereo on all night for their pets.)

If you've ever had an absolutely miserable roommate experience in a small apartment, you'll appreciate just how unpleasant these things could be for all your pets.

Each species needs a dedicated enclosure. If the animals show every indication of getting along well, they can share a play pen for time outside their cages.

Exclusive Free Offer – How to Join

Join other Degu lovers in our unique **FREE** club – Exclusive to owners of this book.

It's quick and easy to sign up. You can receive discounts on Degu food, supplies and more including connecting with other owners. Here's how in 2 simple steps…

Step 1

Go to http://www.DeguBook.com
Enter your name and email address and click 'Join.'

Step 2

Confirm your subscription. As soon as you sign up, we'll send you an email asking you to confirm the details are correct. Just click the link in the email and you'll be joined free.

If you don't receive the email, please check your spam folder and that you used the correct email address.

It's as easy as that. Any questions please email support@degubook.com and where possible, we will help.

Chapter 2 – Buying a Degu

Although degus are becoming more readily available, they are still more difficult to find than other companion rodents like guinea pigs, chinchillas, hamsters, gerbils, and rats.

In larger metropolitan areas, it may be possible to find degus in pet stores, or to work with the store manager to place a special order.

At the back of this book I have included some online sources to purchase degus that were accurate at the time of this writing.

Several are classified lists where hobbyist breeders advertise small numbers of degus on an intermittent basis. Sites of this nature change daily in many cases, so you will want to monitor listings closely.

I also recommend that you join degu enthusiast forums. It is extremely rare for these communities to allow listings of live animals for sale. They are, however, good places to find word-of-mouth referrals to breeders or available litters.

A word on forum etiquette – get to know the "lay" of the land before diving into a discussion. Forums have "cultures" of their own and you can give offense without meaning to simply because you are a "newbie."

Frankly, I am not a big fan of shipping live animals. It is, in my opinion cruel, and stressful. If a shipment is delayed, or if there is a freak weather incident, tragedy is almost always the inevitable result.

I highly encourage you to locate a degu within driving range of your home and to pick up your pet in person. For one thing, you will want to see the animal in advance and verify that it is in good health.

Many of the enthusiast forums also have listings for degus that need to be placed in new homes for many reasons. I always advocate these "rescue" adoptions if at all possible.

Since degus live longer than most companion rodents, you are not short-changing yourself on time spent with your pet and in all likelihood you will be saving a life.

Even using the vast resources of the Internet, however, you may have a hard time finding a degu, so be prepared to be a little patient. These little creatures are definitely worth the wait.

What to Know Before You Buy

Before you purchase your degu, consider each of the following points carefully to ensure that the little animal is a good choice as your companion. Ask yourself the hard questions BEFORE you bring a living creature into your household.

It's important to make sure that your new pet will fit into your lifestyle and living arrangements, and that you can give this clever little animal the time, attention, and care it deserves.

While degus are not especially needy pets, they are highly affectionate and they do need the emotional engagement of their human. This is especially true if you have a single degu housed alone.

Longer Lifespan

Remember that degus have a life expectancy that is longer than most rodents. Although the average is around 8 years, some have been known to live as long as 13 years.

Low Maintenance but Need More Space

As caged pets go, the degu is low maintenance, with cage cleaning typically a once-a-week chore. However, they do require more space than the average pet rodent.

Not Demanding, but Need Socialization

Degus are not demanding, but they do need to be held and played with every day to maintain their socialization and to keep them from becoming lonely.

Need Exercise and Lots of Chew Toys

An exercise wheel is an absolute must for a degu to make sure your pet gets enough exercise. The best type will be solid, with no rungs to catch your pet's tiny feet or cause sores to form. You'll be shocked and delighted at just how far a degu will run in place every day!

You'll also be buying lots and lots and lots of chew toys. A degu's teeth continue to grow throughout its life, so you must provide a means for your pet to keep its dental work worn down.

Specific Dietary Needs

Degus are prone to developing diabetes and cataracts. They must NOT be feed sugary foods. It's important to follow all dietary recommendations for this species to the letter. (See the section on diet and nutrition for more information.)

How to Tell if a Degu is Healthy

When you are examining a degu for potential purchase, look at the conditions in which the animal is being kept. Are the cages clean, well lit, and well ventilated?

Do the degus have adequate space and enough objects to increase intellectual stimulation? Ask how the animals have been socialized and how often they have direct human interaction.

Pay special attention to the following health checks:

Eyes

Look at the degu's eyes. They should be open fully with no discharge present. A healthy degu has shiny, alert eyes that are dark with no white showing and no red spots evident, which can be a sign of developing cataract or retinal issues.

Feet

Ask to see the bottoms of the degu's feet to check for any evidence of sores or open wounds, which are a sign of "bumblefoot."

This is especially important if the degus are being housed in cages with wire floors. If you purchase a degu that has been kept in a habitat with a mesh floor, monitor the condition of its feet carefully for the first few weeks.

Make sure the habitat you design for your pet has plenty of soft surfaces where the little animal can rest.

Coat

A degu's coat should be shiny with no signs of dry, flaky "dandruff" and no bald spots. The hair should be soft, although the tail is bristled at the tip.

A degu that has not had regular access to dust baths will have a coat that is dull and unhealthy in appearance. The hair will also feel "tacky" to the touch.

Teeth

Gently lift the degu's upper lip and then pull down the lower to look at the incisors. The teeth should meet properly with no chips or broken areas.

A degu with teeth that are not properly aligned can still be adopted, but you will be faced with making sure the incisors are clipped back on a routine basis.

With instruction from a veterinary professional, this is a procedure you can perform on your own.

A degu's teeth should be bright orange in color. Although the lurid shade may seem startling, it's perfectly normal and healthy!

Demeanor

By nature degus are alert and curious. An animal that squeaks repeatedly and tries to run away and hide is likely suffering from a high level of stress.

Finally, ask what the degus are being fed to make sure they have not become accustomed to a diet with too much sugar content, which will increase their risk of developing diabetes.

(See the separate sections on diet and nutrition and health problems for more information.)

Day One with Your Degu

At first, your degu will be afraid of you. This is perfectly natural. Don't push the introductions! Give your degu time to get used to the transition to a new home, and think about how the move looks from the animal's perspective.

Every time you put your hand in the cage and try to pick up your pet by essentially cornering it, you look like one thing in the degu's mind — a predator!

Take it slow! On the first day let the little animal just look around its new habitat and explore. Of course you'll want to play with the degu, but resist the urge. Peek in the room, speak to your new pet softly, but don't do anything to stress the degu or frighten it.

After 24 hours, open the cage door and put your hand inside, but don't reach for your pet. Let the degu come to you and give you the "sniff test." Hold out a small treat (just a bit of your pet's regular food, no sweets!)

Over the course of the next few days, only give your degu a treat as a reward when he puts his forepaws up on your hand.

The first "lesson" you want your pet to learn is stepping up onto your open hand. While this is not a "trick" per se, it will make handling your pet much easier and safer.

Allowing the degu to come to you is the best possible way to "pick up" your pet. Degus do not like to be picked up by being grasped around the middle. That feels too much like being restrained or "caught."

The great thing about degus is how easily they adapt to you once they've made that first step on to your hand. Before you know it, your pet will be walking right up your arm to your shoulder.

After a few weeks of this kind of gentle and progressive handling, your degu will come to you willingly and thoroughly enjoy being held — on his own terms!

Degu Proofing

Any time you are allowing a companion animal that is normally caged to have free time out in your home, pick an area that is easy to clean.

Degus, however, are fastidiously clean little animals. They will pick a spot in their cage to urinate and defecate. Needless to say, this makes things considerably easier for their housekeeping staff – you!

If you leave the door to their habitat open while they are enjoying free time, they'll go back in their cage if they need to relieve themselves.

Your little pet will scent mark a room, which involves the secretion of a small amount of urine. Typically this only happens the first time the animal is introduced to a new area. There's no way to get around this natural instinct.

If your degu does eliminate outside the cage, you can be assured he'll go back to the same spot over and over again. Once you've identified your pet's area of preference, it's easy to lay down some kind of protection for your flooring.

Choose a Limited Space

Since degus are small and like to wriggle into tight places, choose a limited space in your home so you can control your pet's comings and goings. If you choose a bathroom, be sure to put the toilet lid down so your degu doesn't fall in.

You should never leave a degu unattended during free play time. They are insatiably curious and can get themselves into all kinds of trouble.

Since time out of the cage is an excellent opportunity to bond with your pet, stay close by and interact with the degu while also keeping him safe from himself!

Close all windows and doors, and make sure no other pets in the house can gain access to the area while your degu is playing.

Check for Toxic Hazards

Check to make sure that your degu can't get into any area where toxic household chemicals are stored. Also, remove any and all houseplants from the play area.

Don't allow your degu to chew on anything plastic. Not only can the material be potentially toxic, it's also a significant choking hazard.

Secure Cords and Cables

Get all electrical cords or cables inside cord minders or otherwise out of your degu's reach. Remember, your pet is a rodent with a natural urge to chew, and is therefore at risk for accidental electrocution.

If you can possibly allow your degus access to an area with no cords present at all, that's the ideal arrangement -- for you and for them.

Appliances

Degus like warm, confined spaces. If you allow your pet to play near electrical appliances, like a clothes dryer, you are running a significant risk of your pet crawling into a dangerous area.

This is especially important if one of your pets has escaped. Check the dryer before starting it! Also, do not vacuum if you have an escaped degu. They are small enough to be sucked into a hose attachment.

Beware of any mechanical pieces of furniture, like recliners or rocking chairs. Anything with an active mechanism is a potential crushing hazard.

Provide Safe Chewing Options

Always give your degus safe wooden toys, cardboard boxes, or egg cartons to play with while they're outside their cage. These items serve a two-fold purpose.

Chew toys keep your pet occupied and away from things you'd rather they leave alone. Due to their small size, they're not as destructive as a chinchilla or a rabbit, but they can get themselves into a great deal of trouble.

These same items serve as necessary intellectual stimulation. Degus are very bright, but they get bored easily. It's actually a good idea to have a big selection of toys that you rotate through different play times.

Get Creative with Intellectual Stimulation

Try to be creative with arrangements and constructions. In the wild, degus dig burrows with interconnecting tunnels, so some lengths of PVC pipe make excellent toys for your pets.

The material is hard enough that they won't be able to chew on it and run the risk of swallowing the pieces. Be sure the pipe is large enough for your pet to pass through each length unhindered.

Think of PVC pipe as "building blocks" for your pet's playground. Buy connecting joints you can use to form a maze of tunnels. Your degus will feel like they're right at home!

Get Down to Eye-Level

When you think you have the area degu proof, take the final precaution of getting down to your pet's eye level and looking again.

When viewed from his perspective, there may be all kinds of fascinating -- and dangerous -- items you've missed. Even a stray corner of wallpaper will attract your degu's attention.

You are trying to keep your pet safe, but also to minimize destruction to your home. When a degu chews, he's not being "bad," he's just being a degu. Chewing is part of his nature. It's up to you to limit his options.

Whatever you don't see in a room, your degu will spot and will check out, so be thorough! This includes any potential "open" doors and windows. Just because you can't fit through, doesn't mean your tiny pet can't!

Chapter 3 – Supplies for Daily Degu Care

Degus are not labor-intensive pets, but they do have definite requirements for housing and daily supplies including proper nutrition.

Any time you acquire a pet of any species, always shop for their "stuff" before you bring your new companion home. Since degus spend most of their time in their habitat, it's especially important that their "house" be completely ready to move in on day one.

Having everything in place also minimizes the stress of the transition to a different environment. This can make all the difference in how quickly your pet will settle down and get used to its life with you and your family.

Designing a Home for Your Degu

In selecting a habitat for your degus, remember that these little guys are really active! They love to run, jump, and climb. The absolute minimum size enclosure for a pair of degus is:

- 27.5 inches / 70 cm long
- 18 inches / 46 cm wide
- 39 inches / 99 cm high

Always think height over length. Degus like a tall cage much better than a long one. They thoroughly enjoy getting up high and observing everything that's going on in their world.

The best wisdom for any small animal habitat, however, is to buy the largest enclosure you can afford and for which you have adequate room in your home.

For a cage that falls within or exceeds the recommended minimum size budget $150-$300 / £94-£188.

Types of Cages

It is highly unlikely that you will find a cage that is made specifically for a degu. Instead, you'll be shopping for other small animal cages that will meet both the needs of your new pet and your own budget and available space.

Note that many cages can be purchased online for less money, but you may want to visit some large pet stores and really examine cage types before you make your final decision.

You can see some degu cages here
www.DeguBook.com/cages.htm (USA)
www.DeguBook.com/cagesuk.htm (UK)

Small Animal and Bird Cages

Almost any cage that is appropriate for a chinchilla will also work well for a degu. Typically these units are constructed from either stainless steel or galvanized mesh panels.

Ferret cages are generally even larger and have nice big doors and deep bases. You want a habitat with a very deep pan or base to hold substrate. Also, make sure there are plenty of points of attachment for accessories like shelves, branches, and hammocks.

If a cage has been constructed specifically for rats, the material is generally covered in a protective layer of powdered enamel.

Rat cages are typically multi-level and may be more flexible in terms of multiple forms of configuration and arrangement.

Birdcages, especially those made for large parrots, can be very spacious. Don't get bars that are spaced more than an inch (2.54 cm) wide or you'll be inviting an untimely escape!

You will likely need to do more accessorizing with a birdcage, but these units are durable and will last a long time. They also provide excellent ventilation.

Aquariums Are Temporary Options Only

Many small pets are housed in glass "aquariums" or vivariums. These tanks work really well for hamsters and gerbils, but they're not going to work for a degu for anything more than a temporary expedient, and then only when the animal is small.

If, however, a mesh cage "topper" is added to create a tall, ventilated area, this is a potential option. Any such unit is a custom design, however, and if not well considered, will be difficult to clean or to move.

Do not make the mistake of thinking you can house a degu in an aquarium for life. The area is too small and the solid sides won't provide good airflow for your pet.

Points to Remember in Cage Selection

As you are examining the features of any cage, remember all the following:

- Never get anything with a plastic base on which your pets can gnaw.

- Make sure doors and openings are large enough for your degus to easily fit through.

- Don't get a mesh floor. Degus can easily break their legs if they get a foot caught in the mesh, and the wires are hard on their feet. (See the chapter on health to read about "bumblefoot" or pododermatitis.)

When you are looking at any habitat for purchase, always think in terms of potential jailbreaks.

Degus aren't necessarily trying to get out, but if there's a hole they can squeeze through, they will. It's simply in their nature.

Time Outside the Cage

As you contemplate housing space for your degus, please realize they will also need time outside their enclosure, either in a large playpen or in a room you've made "degu proof." (Please refer to Chapter 2 where I discuss this process.)

Degus need both exercise and intellectual stimulation in an area where they feel safe to explore and check things out.

They'll be even happier if they get to interact with you while they're doing it. At the very least, plan on half an hour a day outside the cage for your little pets.

Habitat Placement

Never position your degu's habitat in direct sunlight. Remember that in the wild the degu retreats to its burrow during the hottest hours of the day.

The ideal room temperature for degus is 70° F / 21° C. A variation of a couple of degrees in either direction is not a cause for alarm, but do not allow the temperature in your degu's habitat to swing wildly between extremes.

Don't subject your little pets to drafts and cold spots, which put them in danger of contracting pneumonia. Be especially careful that young degus don't get too cold.

Position the habitat at waist level or higher. This will give you ease of access and a clear line of sight to watch your pets play.

Degus like to be able to get up high to see what's going on and they don't like to feel they're being "loomed" over. Your pet should be able to reach you at eye level in some portion of its habitat.

Consider a Playpen

Using a playpen is an excellent way to keep your degus safe and to allow them more time in and out of the cage.

If you can position the cage in a corner, you may even be able to designate a permanent enlarged play area outside your pet's primary home using wire panels as "fencing."

Since degus will normally return to their habitat to use their preferred spot for urination and defecation, an arrangement of this kind can be ideal.

Make sure, however, that you use panels with mesh small enough that your pet cannot wriggle through or get caught. The material should be stainless steel or galvanized metal, not plastic.

Make the playpen large enough for you to be inside with your pets during play hours. This is an excellent alternative to degu-proofing an entire room and works particularly well for apartment dwellers with limited space.

Make sure the panels are at least 6 feet / 1.8 meters tall or higher and are securely anchored. If you have no other pets in the house, you may be able to use slightly shorter panels, but remember that degus climb very well.

Since you may have to have panels fabricated to achieve a good playpen arrangement, it's difficult to place an estimated price on this arrangement.

Collapsible playpens that are designed for ferrets or rabbits start at around $50 / £31, but these may not be appropriate for your pet or your living circumstances.

Small Travel Crate

There may be times when you will need to transport your degus, or to confine them to a small area during cage cleaning.

A small pet carrier suitable for use with a cat or dog will work fine for a degu, but find one that is made of stainless steel, not plastic.

Travel crates made of stainless steel are used primarily for small dogs. Make sure the bar placement is safe for your degu. You should budget around $50 / £31 to find a suitable unit.

If you are forced to buy a travel crate with plastic components, don't leave your degus inside for any extended period of time.

When your degus are in their crate, always give them plenty of toys to keep them occupied. Otherwise, they'll start gnawing on the crate itself. This raises the potential for a "jailbreak," and also creates a choking danger.

Diet and Nutrition

The fundamental components of your degu's diet are grass hay and pellets formulated for chinchillas or guinea pigs. Add some fresh vegetables for variety, and as treats.

As you will read in the chapter on health, degus often develop diabetes. It's essential not to let your pet get overweight and to feed a diet with a high amount of roughage and few carbohydrates.

Like any pet, degus love things that aren't good for them, and easily develop a "sweet tooth." Do not let this kind of dietary behavior get started! The health consequences for your pet are dangerous and often irreversible.

www.DeguBook.com/food.htm (USA)
www.DeguBook.com/fooduk.htm (UK)

Good Quality Hay

Using good quality grass hay like timothy will provide your degu with the roughage its system needs while keeping your pet's teeth ground down. Make hay available for your degus at all times.

Buy a small hay rack that will attach to the side of the cage. You can find these racks online or in pet stores for approximately $8 / £5.

Even if you use a rack, the degu will scatter the hay. Remove loose and soiled hay daily, placing fresh hay in the rack. Never let your pet run out of hay. It is the primary component of his diet and the cornerstone of good health.

Good quality hay smells clean and dry and does not appear dusty or dull. Make sure there is no debris like thorns or burrs in the mixture.

Good choices for grass hays include:

- Timothy
- Mountain grass
- Brome
- Orchard grass

Alfalfa is an option 2-3 times a week as it is a good source of calcium, but don't overdo it. The pellet feed you select will likely have alfalfa as a primary ingredient.

Timothy hay is available pre-packaged to feed small animals. It comes in a range of sizes from 5-50 lbs / 2.27-22.7 kg and sells for $20-$65 / £12-£40.

Hay Cubes May Be Used

Timothy hay compressed into cubes is sold by the package at pet stores. These cubes can be a highly convenient option as they are less messy than loose hay. Typically, the cubes are broken into small chunks and served in a food bowl.

Just like loose hay, make sure the cubes stay dry and are stored in a vented container to prevent the growth of mold. All hay should be kept in a cool, dry place out of the sun.

Compressed timothy hay cubes are priced at $14 / £9 per 6 lb. / 2.7 kg.

www.DeguBook.com/hay.htm (USA)
www.DeguBook.com/hayuk.htm (UK)

Pellet Foods *Not* Mix

Because degus are prone to both diabetes and cataracts, it is important that their diet not contain either molasses or sugar. There are other serious cautions to consider in picking a pellet food.

Unsafe Pellet Mixes

Do NOT give your pet rabbit pellets or mix. These feeds often contain coccidiostat drugs added to the mix to prevent the spread of coccidiosis, a bacterial infection. These drugs are toxic to degus.

Additionally, rabbit food doesn't have the right vitamin and mineral levels degus require. Hamster and gerbil food have a high seed content that renders them unsuitable for use with degus because the overall fat and protein levels in the mix are too great.

Safe Pellet Mixes

It is perfectly safe to feed your pet pellets that have been formulated for chinchillas or guinea pigs, but they should *not* receive a mix that includes fruit. Feed straight pellets only.

An adult degu should be fed about 0.35 ounces / 9.9 grams of pellet food per day. Do NOT leave pellets out all the time. Your degu will come to prefer these feeds and won't consume enough hay to keep their digestive systems and teeth in good shape.

There are degu-specific pellets available including:

- Sunseed Vita Degu Formula, 28 oz, $7 (US)
- Exotic Nutrition Degu Complete Diet, 10 lbs, $24 (US)
- Degu Nuggets, 2 kg, £4.75 (UK)
- Science Selective Degu, 350g, £2.59 (UK)

If you can only find chinchilla pellets, consider the following:

- In the United States, Oxbow Chinchilla Deluxe pellets 5-50 lbs, $11 - $50.

- In the UK, Charnwood Pellets, 5 kg, £5.38.

Appropriate guinea pig formulations include Gerty Guinea Pig ($7 / £4) and Excel Guinea ($8 / £5).

Vitamin C Supplement

Vitamin C is an important supplement for your degu, working to make its immune system healthier and playing a role in the prevention of heart disease, cancers, and cataracts.

To ensure that your pet is getting adequate Vitamin C, you can add powder to the daily pellet food ration (crushing a regular Vitamin C tablet is fine.)

You can also give your degu fresh vegetable "treats" high in Vitamin C content. These foods include:
- Broccoli
- Red peppers
- Parsley
- Rosehips

Rosehip powder sprinkled on the pellet food is also a good option since the substance is naturally sweet.

Feeding Fresh Vegetables

Fresh vegetables will give your degu that level of amino acids and fatty acids that it requires to stay healthy. Fruits, however, should be severely restricted due to their sugar content – just a bite or two once a month.

Be careful in selecting greens for your pet, however, as some will cause bloat. Be especially sparing with cabbage, peas, and lettuce for this reason.

Most other vegetable types are safe. Degus take the "herb" in herbivore seriously and absolutely love parsley, mint, and basil.

Don't overdo with any of these foods however. Give a few bits, no larger than your thumbnail, 1-2 times each week.

Vegetables that can be safely fed on a weekly basis include:

- Butternut squash
- Red and green peppers
- Spring onions
- Beet root
- Radishes

Vegetables to feed in moderation include:

- Cabbage
- Green beans
- Carrot tops
- Cauliflower leaves and stalk
- Leeks
- Broccoli
- Celery
- Asparagus
- Lettuce
- Brussels sprouts

Feed the following items only once a month:

- Sweet corn
- Cherry tomatoes
- Apples
- Cucumbers
- Sweet potatoes
- Peas
- Carrots

Always alternate vegetable types to give your pet some variety and to lessen the chance of incidents of bloating. Obviously the price of fresh produce varies by location and season.

One good thing about this aspect of your pet's diet is that you can buy the produce for yourself and just share a little with your degu.

Food and Water Containers

Use ceramic or earthenware bowls for your degu's food. They'll chew on plastic, and tip the bowls over because they're too light. You can also select stainless steel bowls that attach to the side of the cage.

Earthenware or ceramic bowls are priced at $20-$30 / £13-£19, while stainless steel units cost $10-$15 / £6-£9.

Just as a hint, if you have two degus, get two food bowls or be prepared for a shoving match at meal times!

Opt for a glass water bottle with a stainless steel, ball bearing "lixit" tip. These bottles are very efficient and they ensure a constant source of clean water. Position the spout at the level of your pet's mouth.

For a 16-ounce / 0.47 liter water bottle you'll pay $18-$20 / £11-£13.

Accessorizing the Habitat

Buying accessories for your degu's cage is a vital part of caring for your pet. Accessories and toys provide both exercise and intellectual enrichment.

An Exercise Wheel is a Must

Degus absolutely adore their exercise wheels, running for such long periods of time you'd swear they'd drop from exhaustion at any moment.

Degus are capable of running more than 2.5 miles / 4 km a day! This not only keeps them well occupied, but it ensures that your pet does not become obese.

Buy a wheel that is at least 10-12 inches (25-30 cm) in diameter at a width of 4 inches (10 cm). For a pair of degus, you really should have two wheels, even though that will mean a much bigger cage.

The wheel should be solid, not made with rungs. A solid wheel is much safer for your pet's feet, ensuring that the degu doesn't slip and break a limb or develop sores on the feet.

A large exercise wheel with a solid track will cost $20-$25 / £13-£16.

A Nest Box "Burrow"

In captivity, a nest box becomes a degu's "burrow." This small box will allow your pet to hide and grab some private time, and to nap snuggled away in a secure spot.

Pick a box that will accommodate your total number of degus. They should be able to stand on all fours and turn around while they are inside. The box should have a removable top for ease of cleaning.

Nest boxes may be made of wood or metal and are priced from $30 / £19 and up. Usually they can be attached to the side of the cage for greater stability.

Use hay, paper towels, or shredded paper for bedding. Degus are especially fond of small pet tent hammocks.

These units, which look like tiny camping tents, are suspended in the cage. They come in a range of sizes and sell for $7-$15 / £4-£9.

If you get a hammock – and really, there's nothing cuter than a degu peeking out the tent hole at you – position it in a corner to give your pet a maximum sense of security.

Selecting a Cage Substrate

Choosing a material or substrate to line the bottom of your degu's cage is a matter of personal preference — yours and your pet's!

You want to pick something that will let you keep the habitat clean, but also please your degu who, after all, has to live in the stuff.

The products below all vary in price, but as an example, a 2.1 cubic feet / 59.5 liter package of pine shavings costs $18 / £11.

Pine Shavings

Pine shavings that have been kiln dried are reasonably absorbent and do a good job of keeping odors in check. The material is cheap and can be composted, plus it has some anti-bacterial properties.

If, however, you are allergic to wood dust, pine shavings can be a problem. Also, they are feather light. If your degu has a fit of kicking the shavings, they're going to go everywhere.

Paper Bedding

Paper bedding products are fairly new on the market and are made from recycled materials. This is a positive for the environmentally minded pet owner, plus there's a low dust factor.
One drawback to paper is that while the material is highly absorbent, it's also really heavy when wet and can be hard to clean out of the cage. Paper bedding can also be composted. This material is, however, a pricey option.

(Simply using shredded newspaper is not recommended. Although modern inks are classified as "safe," there is still a risk of toxicity for your pet.)

Hay or Straw

It's certainly possible to just use piles of fresh hay in the bottom of the cage, but the material is not absorbent and will mold quite easily. If you use hay, you should clean out the soiled material daily.

In terms of intellectual enrichment, hay is certainly fun for degus since they'll burrow in and nest to their heart's content, plus the hay is edible for your pet.

If you live in a rural area and have a constant supply of clean, fresh hay this can be a good option, just be prepared for somewhat higher maintenance.

Substrates Not to Use

Although you will see cedar shavings by the bagful in pet stores, do NOT use them with degus. Cedar is highly toxic to your pet.

Also avoid any cat litter pellets that are wood based. Your degus may eat the litter and be subject to dangerous bowel impaction and blockages.

It's completely possible for your pet to be allergic to any kind of substrate, so if you notice your degu sneezing, try changing to a different type of bedding.

Dust Bath

Degus, like chinchillas, bathe in dust rather than water. When given a tray of specially formulated dust, your little pet will roll to his heart's content and kick up a happy mess while he's doing it.

To find the right dust for your degu, just buy a commercial chinchilla dust like Kaytee Chinchilla Dust Bath for $10 / £6 (2.5 lbs / 1.13 kg).

Don't give your pet more than a few spoons of dust in a good-sized tray, preferably with sides to help contain the mess. You can also shop for a chinchilla bath "house," which is an even tidier option.

After each bath, throw out the used dust and start fresh next time. This process will keep your degu's coat from getting greasy and also provides protection against parasites.

www.DeguBook.com/dust.htm (USA)
www.DeguBook.com/dustuk.htm (UK)

Toys, Toys, and More Toys

When it comes to toys, degus are rather like children. They get bored with what they have and are always on the lookout for something new. One way to get around this is to invest in a good selection of toys and rotate the items in and out of the habitat.

Some of the toys can be "homemade." Stuff an old paper towel or toilet tissue cardboard roll with hay and maybe hide a single treat in the middle.

Your degus will pretty well shred the tube to get to the goodies, but they'll be completely absorbed in the process!

Other options include:

- Rope toys made of cotton or sisal
- Any kind of sisal chew toy
- Climbing branches (apple, hazel, dried pine, hawthorn)
- Wooden blocks and chew sticks
- Logs
- Tunnels made of PVC pipe

Really, anything that catches your pet's attention, is non-toxic, not made of plastic, and doesn't raise a choking danger is fair game.

Training Your Degu

Like many rodents, degus are highly intelligent and capable of following simple logical sequences to complete fairly complex tasks.

In some research studies, degus have even learned to use rudimentary tools. They have also proven to be able to stack objects in order of ascending or descending size, a level of reasoning once believed only possible for apes.

Follow Recommended Best Practices

With any companion animal, training is about trust. You should never try to force an animal to do anything. The entire system works on positive and negative feedback, with the "negative" being nothing more than your pet not being given a reward.

Do not allow training treats to throw your degu off its diet, however. The only "special" items that are acceptable are things like a bit of natural puffed rice, a single piece of corn, bread crumbs, or single oats.

Because degus are extremely affectionate with their owners, verbal praise, petting, and a nice tummy rub can all be used as positive reinforcement. You may be surprised by just how eager your pet is to please you.

Be extremely patient. All degus are individuals and they do not all learn at the same rate.

Tap Training

Degus will typically respond to the sound of finger tapping on a flat surface. This is an excellent way to teach your pet its name. The sequence is quite simple

- Tap with your finger.

- Reward your degu when it comes to you.

When your pet consistently responds to the finger tap, start using its name:

- "Squeaky."
- Tap, tap, tap.

- Dispense the treat when the degu comes to you.

After several days, take the tap out of the sequence.

- "Squeaky."
- Dispense the treat when the degu comes to you.

Before long, you won't need to use the treat at all to get the degu to respond to its name, and you can always add the finger tap back if you need to really get your pet's attention.

Since the finger tap has become a recognized attention getter, you can use that device to extrapolate on things your pet can do on "command."

For instance, get a tube of some sort that is degu-sized. A length of PVC pipe will work quite well. Get your degu's attention and then tap on the tube.

- "Squeaky."
- Tap on the tube.
- Reward the degu when it approaches to investigate.

As soon as your pet approaches the tube on command, tap at the other end of the tube. Remember that degus are burrowing animals. It will be quite natural in your pet's mind to go through the tube rather than around it.
- "Squeaky."
- Tap on the far end of the tube.
- Reward the degu when it goes through the tube and comes to you.

Use the same progression of commands until you can call the degu through the tube and to you. Since degus will pick up verbal commands, you can add a secondary command to your pet's name and create an entire training language.

Instead of just saying "Squeaky" to initiate the tube "trick," you might say, "Squeaky, tunnel."

Observation and Extrapolation

The most effective training is born of watching your pet for what the degu likes to do naturally and then building those behaviors into trick sequences. Use the same combination of verbal cues and taps, always with positive rewards.

Degus like to interact with their humans, and they will quickly figure out that the whole business is a game that earns them rewards.

Don't be surprised to see your little pet mixing up the sequences and inventing new tricks to "show" you in order to up their ratio of positive, edible reinforcements!

Cage Maintenance

By nature, degus are clean to the point of being fastidious. They appreciate a clean cage. Since they don't produce large amounts of urine, you'll only need to spot clean on a daily basis and do a major cleaning once a week.

Replace all of the substrate and wipe down all the surfaces in the cage including ladders, bowls, shelves, and toys. Don't forget to also put fresh bedding in the nest box.

Use warm water and vinegar. Don't use any cleaner with harsh chemicals and make sure everything is completely rinsed off and dry before you return your pet to the enclosure.

Once a month, take the cage completely apart and give everything a thorough scrubbing. Put the components outside in the sun to air out and dry.

During this period you can either let your degus have playtime in a safe area, or let them hang out in their travel crate.

Estimated Costs

Degus:

$20-$40 / £13-£25 per individual
$40-$80 / £25-£50 or less per pair

Cage:

For a cage that falls within or exceeds the recommended minimum size of:

- 27.5 inches / 69.9 cm long
- 18 inches / 46 cm wide

- 39 inches / 99 cm high

$150-$300 / £94-£188

Collapsible Playpen:

$50 / £31

(Note that these units, which are designed for ferrets and rabbits, may not be appropriate for your degu or fit your living circumstances.)

Travel Crate:

$50 / £31

Make sure the unit you select has as little exposed plastic as possible. If possible, buy a stainless steel crate.
Hay Rack:

$8 / £5

Grass Hay:

Packaged timothy hay 5-50 lbs / 2.27-22.68 kg
$20-$65 / £12-£40

Compressed timothy hay cubes
are priced at $14 / £9 per 6 lbs / 2.72 kg

Pellet Foods:

Each of the following pellet foods is a safe and nutritionally appropriate food for use with your degus. Note, do not use rabbit pellets with your degu.

Sunseed Vita Degu Formula, 28 oz, $7 (US)

Exotic Nutrition Degu Complete Diet, 10 lbs, $24 (US)

Degu Nuggets, 2 kg, £4.75 (UK)

Science Selective Degu, 350g, £2.59 (UK)

Oxbow Chinchilla Deluxe pellets 5-50 lbs, $11 - $50 (US)

Charnwood Pellets, 5 kgs, £5.38 (UK)

Gerty Guinea Pig, $7 / £4

Excel Guinea, $8 / £5

Fresh Vegetables:

The price of fresh produce varies by location and season. You can buy produce for yourself and share a little with your degu.

Food Bowls:

Earthenware or ceramic bowls, $20-$30 / £13-£19
Stainless steel units, $10-$15 / £6-£9

Water Bottle with "lixit" Spout:

16-ounce / 0.5 liter water bottle, $18-$20 / £11-£13

Exercise Wheel:

Large wheel with a solid track, $20-$25 / £13-£16

Nest Box:

$7-$15 / £4-£9

(Nest boxes come in varying sizes. Buy according to the number of degus you are keeping as they will sleep together.)

Pine Shavings Substrate:

2.1 cubic feet / 59.5 liter package
$18 / £11

Dust Bath:

Kaytee Chinchilla Dust Bath
2.5 lbs / 1.13 kg - $10 / £6

Total Estimated Costs:

$450 / £281 - $650 / £406

Quick Facts: Learn to Speak Degu

Degus are excellent communicators with one another and eventually with you as soon as you understand their vocabulary, which is comprised of sounds and body language.

Pilo-Erection

This is a fancy term for a degu's hair being raised. It can mean a number of things from, "I don't like that!" to "That's scary!" Also, when two degus are playing, you may see one raise its hair before pouncing good-naturedly on its friend.

As a defensive measure against predators, the degu raises its hairs in an effort to make itself look larger and somewhat more "threatening." While this may work with other degus, it really isn't much of a defense against serious predators.

Tail Wagging

When a degu takes off running, they hold their tails up like bushy little flags. Tail wagging, however, can mean everything from, "I'm in a really good mood," to "check that out!" or even, "Hey, wanna go on a date?"

It's always best to gauge the overall situation before you decide what your degu's tail wag actually means. For instance if there has been some sort of confrontation, the degu's body may tremble a little and its tail may wag indicating either its satisfaction at being dominant, or its capitulation to the submissive role.

Play Behaviors

Degus play enthusiastically and exhibit a range of play-associated behaviors that include full-out running, exuberant jumping, comical hopping, and sort of twisting, mid-air leaps.

All of these behaviors mean pretty much the same thing, "This is fun!"

Other "Vocabulary"

Other things you may see your degu doing, or hear him "saying" include:

- Grooming you or another degu - "Friends for life!"

- Scent marking - "Mine, all mine!"

- Growling - "Back off, buddy!"

- Squealing - "Enough, already!" or "Ouch!"

- Chuckling - "Kids! Get over here!"

- Tooth chatter - "You are on my last nerve cell!"

Degus also engage in comical shoving matches that are really nothing more than posturing. Just imagine one degu saying to the other, "Oh yeah? Well, your whiskers look funny!"

Chuck Wee

The "chuck wee" is a specialized call peculiar to the degu. The sound doesn't mean your pet is frightened, just that it is in a state of interested alertness.

The "chuck wee" is hard to describe. It begins with a slightly garbled "cluck," that progresses to a buzzing chuckle.

You may hear a chuck wee when your degu sees you coming and is excited. In this setting the sound is a definite happy greeting and an interested, "Hey! What are we going to do now?"

Chapter 4 – Degu Health and Breeding

Although degus are prone to certain medical conditions, they are normally quite healthy and hardy. The key to your degu's wellbeing is a proper diet and excellent cage maintenance.

They do not require vaccinations, and many go their entire lives never crossing the threshold of a vet's office. The following are the major issues and conditions most prevalent in this species.

This material is intended as a health overview only and is not meant to take the place of a consultation with a qualified veterinary professional.

Spaying and Neutering

In animals this small, if you wish to keep a male and female pair but do not want them to reproduce, it's much better to neuter the male than to attempt to spay the female.

The neutering process for males is much faster and less invasive, and does not require a lengthy period under anesthesia. It is recommended, however, that a male be at least a year old before the procedure is performed.

(Note that it is sometimes necessary to neuter males kept together to curb aggression.)

Dental Health

The vast majority of degus taken to vet clinics have issues with their teeth. If your degus don't get enough hay to grind down their molars and incisors, which continue to grow throughout their lives, they may experience painful dental conditions.

If their molars overgrow and develop sharp, pointed "spurs," the cheeks and tongue may become lacerated. Cuts in the mouth are easily subject to infection.

Overly long incisors can prevent your degu from being able to eat at all.

Watch your pets closely for signs of dental issues that will include:

- Pawing or worrying at the mouth
- Apparent discomfort when eating
- Dropping food
- Loss of appetite
- Weight loss
- Wet drool around the mouth

Your vet will need to examine your pet's teeth. If these problems are present, a light anesthesia will be used to allow the doctor to grind off the spurs and clip back the incisors.

To prevent a recurrence, change your pet's diet to include more hay and increase the degu's access to chew toys.

Clipping Your Degu's Teeth

Although many degu owners pale at the suggestion, it is possible for you to clip your pet's teeth if the animal suffers from a permanent "malocclusion." This is the term for teeth that are crooked or tend to overgrow.

Because the degu may not be able to chew appropriately, maloccluded teeth often do not wear down properly. They can, however, be trimmed throughout your pet's life.

Do NOT attempt to trim your degu's teeth without first being instructed in the procedure by a qualified veterinary professional.

When you understand how to do the clipping, however, the only required equipment is a simple pair of human nail clippers.

Diabetes

A degu's body can't metabolize dietary sugar, making these little animals highly prone to developing diabetes. This places a severe strain on their kidneys. Diabetes is a serious condition, and must not be ignored.

The symptoms of diabetes include:

- Consuming unusually large amounts of water
- A marked increase in urine output
- Cataracts in both eyes

If there are other degus in the cage, you may see them licking the urine because it is sweet.

If your degu is showing signs of diabetes, any foods high in sugars must be immediately eliminated from your pet's diet. There is, unfortunately, no cure for this disease.

Working with your vet, you can, however, manage the condition. Note that this may well involve regular glucose testing of the degu's urine.

The most important step you can take in regard to diabetes is to never let it develop in the first place.

Feed your degu a well-balanced diet that is appropriate for its metabolism with severely limited amounts of sugars present. (See the section on diet and nutrition for more information.)

Cataracts

Because cataracts often appear in conjunction with diabetes, they are fairly common in degus. Sorbitol builds up on the lens of the eye making it cloudy or opaque in appearance, significantly reducing the degu's visual acuity.

Cataracts do occur independently of diabetes and can be an inherited condition. If the cloudiness is present in both eyes, however, you will know your pet has diabetes.

Since the cloudiness is quite visible in the eye, it's not difficult to understand what is happening to your degu's vision. For the most part they learn to cope quite well, relying on their sense of smell and their keen hearing to get around.

There is no cure for cataracts. When you realize that cataracts are developing, simplify the layout of your pet's cage for ease of movement and then don't change anything!

The degu, like any creature with diminished vision, will memorize its surroundings, which will greatly facilitate its ability to continue to lead an enjoyable life.

Be certain when you clean the cage that everything is put back in exactly the same place with the same orientation.

Ear Health

Degus have relatively large ears, but it is typically difficult to see down into the ear canal. Like all animals, degus can be prone to ear mites, infections, and injuries affecting the ears.

If there is an obvious tear or physical injury, seek veterinary assistance. A foul odor emanating from the ears likely indicates the presence of mites.

You will know that your degu's ears are paining or annoying your pet if the animal shakes its head repeatedly, tilts the head to one side, paws at the ears, or seems to be off balance.

Do NOT try to swab out your pet's ears without the assistance of a qualified veterinarian. You can, however, put a little mineral oil on a cotton swab and remove visible debris from the ear flap, which may relieve itching.

If the condition persists, or if your degu's ears smell, you will need to take your pet to the vet to get an appropriate medication.

De-gloving of the Tail

A degu's tail is designed to protect the animal from predators. When restrained by the tail, the appendage simply comes off.

Granted, this is in no way a pretty sight, nor is it pleasant to watch the degu trim down the remaining stump which the degu does instinctively. The wound heals very rapidly, however, and your pet will quickly recalibrate its ability to balance.

When the wound occurs, the tendons and vertebrae are exposed with the skin and hair torn away. Bleeding should stop in about 20 minutes.

Over the next few days the exposed material dries out and the degu chews it away. If there is any additional bleeding, drainage, or swelling, take your pet to the vet.

In order to prevent de-gloving, never handle your pet by the tail and make sure there are no hazards in the cage where the degu's tail could become caught.

Pododermatitis

Pododermatitis, more commonly known as "bumblefoot" causes painful pressure sores on the feet. Walking or standing on mesh surfaces or running in a wheel with rungs can cause this condition.

If your degu is limping or unusually inactive, check the bottoms of the feet for sores. You may find open ulcers that are weeping. These require immediate veterinary attention and the administration of antibiotics.

Immediately remove all rough or uneven surfaces from the cage and pad everything else with towels or reed mats. These will have to be changed and washed frequently until your pet's feet heal to prevent infections.

Follow your vet's instructions to the letter in regard to bathing the feet with saline solution and administering any medications.

It is best with degus to never to use a cage with a mesh base and to make sure all cage surfaces are smooth. Provide some padded areas for sitting and resting other than the nest box.

Gastrointestinal Problems

The major gastrointestinal issues in degus are normally limited to three conditions: constipation, diarrhea, and bloat.

Constipation

Constipation may be caused by a failure to drink enough water, an overly hot environment, some sort of intestinal blockage, or even parasite activity.

If your pet's droppings become hard and dry, remove all dry food except hay and give your pet apple slices and a few green vegetables until the condition improves.

If you do not see the stools returning to normal in a day or two, consult your veterinarian.

Diarrhea

Diarrhea can be a consequence of stress and infection, but typically the condition is directly related to a diet with too much fruit and vegetables over hay and pellet foods.

Because diarrhea can cause life-threatening dehydration, it is important not to ignore this condition. Remove all fruits and vegetables from your pet's diet and consult your veterinarian.

It may be necessary for the vet to administer electrolyte solution intravenously to support your pet's recovery, or for you to give the degu an oral pediatric electrolyte liquid for the same purpose.

Bloat

When gas accumulates in the degu's gastrointestinal tract, this causes an uncomfortable swelling referred to as "bloat." The cause may be an infection (bacterial, viral, or protozoan in origin) or some form of obstruction.

Bloat should be treated as a serious medical emergency. It is extremely important that you get your pet to the vet as soon as possible to relieve both the swelling and the accompanying pain.

Infections

Infections are very difficult to spot and treat in most small animals and degus are no exception. You must realize that these creatures interact with the world from the perspective of prey. They hide their illnesses so as not to appear weak and vulnerable to larger animals.

You will always be your pet's best preventive healthcare plan. Observe and handle your pet daily. Look for any soft lumps on the body that could indicate the presence of an abscess.

Be aware of any brownish, thick discharge from the eyes, or strong smells coming from the ears. Watch for changes in behavior that could range from lethargy to disorientation.

- How is your pet breathing?
- Are the respirations overly rapid?
- Is the degu wheezing or sneezing?
- Is its nose running?
- Is your pet maintaining its body weight?
- Is the degu eating well?

Any of these things could be the sign of a serious infection that would require veterinary intervention. Always err on the side of caution and take your degu to the vet if you think something is wrong.

Dehydration

Any animal can become dehydrated when too much water is lost from its system. In degus this can be a consequence of infection, diarrhea, or heatstroke.

It is important to rehydrate your pet, but do not force water on an animal that is too weak to drink on its own or that is unconscious. Doing so runs the risk of water getting in the lungs.

If your pet is in a weakened or unconscious state, it needs an electrolyte solution administered by a veterinarian professional. If you have no access to a vet, you can use a pediatric electrolyte solution formulated for human babies.

Use an eyedropper and put only a few drops in the degu's mouth until the animal becomes responsive. Do not give your pet water with sugar or salt mixed in, as these will do more harm than good.

Heatstroke

The optimal temperature for a degu is 70° F / 21° C. Never place your pet's cage in direct sunlight or close to any source of heat.

If you are transporting your pet to the vet or to any other location, never leave the degu in the car unless the air conditioning is turned on.

Also, be extremely careful not to allow the travel crate to sit in a sunny spot on the seat. If necessary, put the crate in the foot well between the front and back seats.

Degus suffering from heatstroke weaken quickly and lapse into an unconscious state. It is imperative to gently lower your pet's body temperature.

Hold the degu in your hand and partially submerge your pet in a few inches of cool — not cold — water in the sink. Be very careful to keep the degu's head out of the water.

When the degu regains consciousness, dry your pet gently with a cloth and return it to its cage, lowering the lights in the room.

Make sure your pet has a supply of clean, cool drinking water. You may want to try to get your pet to take a few drops of a pediatric electrolyte solution.

If your pet does not show improvement, immediately seek veterinary assistance.

Physical Trauma

Due to their small size, degus can be seriously injured if they are dropped, mishandled, accidentally stepped on, or have a dangerous interaction with another family pet.

At the very least, these situations will result in serious emotional upset, but there may also be physical injury and even shock. It is important to gently isolate your pet in an area where you can examine it for wounds.

Do not, however, handle the degu any more than is absolutely necessary as you may unwittingly cause additional injury. Speak softly to your pet and observe its demeanor.

If your degu begins to move around normally once its fear subsides, keep your pet in a quiet spot and continue to allow it to recover on its own.

If, however, there are any signs of blood, any indication of physical injury, or if your pet is unresponsive, seek veterinary assistance immediately.

Finding a Veterinarian

Degus are regarded as exotic animals, so you will want to interview veterinarians in your area who are either familiar with the species or willing to learn more about them.

For the most part it's rare for a degu to require veterinary care, but you should have a vet selected even before you bring your pet home.

Most small animal veterinarians are quite capable of treating degus due to their similarity to guinea pigs and chinchillas.

Be prepared to call around, and don't be shy about asking questions. If your vet has experience with other companion rodents, they are in a good position to effectively treat your degu.

Thankfully, these animals are quite healthy if well cared for. A well-maintained cage and a proper diet will go a long way toward keeping your degu in excellent health.
Medication Tolerances

Do not, however, be surprised if you are put in a position of providing information to your veterinarian about your degu. The following medications should be avoided with this species:

- Metoclopramide
- Fusidic acid
- Trimethoprim
- Sulfamethoxazole

If anesthesia is required, degus tolerate both isoflourane and ketamine. They also respond well to most broad spectrum antibiotics.

Breeding Degus

Degus kept as companion animals are typically fully matured by age 53-55 weeks and capable of reproducing at that time.

Mating

In their native habitat, degus breed in September. The females are seasonally fertile, but males are ready to reproduce year round. The female does not ovulate until breeding occurs.

Makes initiate the courtship with a series of behaviors including grooming, nose-to-nose contact, tail wagging, nuzzling, and trembling. He will also spray urine over her back, a process called enurination, which she may reciprocate.

The actual breeding is short, requiring only 5-10 seconds. This is likely an adaption to minimize the degus' vulnerability to predators.

Birth

Females have an unusually long gestation period for a rodent at 90-93 days. The birth will occur inside the nest box, and may take several hours.

Do not try to watch or peek in during this time. You'll frighten and stress the mother.

Litters are typically comprised of about 6 pups. The babies begin suckling within hours and nurse lying on their backs while the mother stands huddled over them.

Degus come into the world with their eyes open and their fur and teeth in place. Within 3-4 hours the pups will be able to stand on their own, walk, sit up on their tiny haunches, and even make vocalization.

Rearing

Although both parents can and will participate in raising their young, it's best to remove the male from the enclosure as soon as the pups are born and to let him bunk on his own for a few days.

This is a precaution to make sure that he does not immediately breed with the female again. After about a week it should be safe to return him to the main habitat.

Even though degu pups look prepared to greet their new world, the pups require a great deal of care from their mother during the first weeks of their lives and should not be separated from her.

In addition to their emotional and nutritional need to be near her, the pups can't regulate their own body temperature and will rely on their mother's warmth until they are about 20 days old.

As adorable as the babies will be, they should not be handled because the stress is simply too great for them. At birth, they will weigh about 14.6 grams and will add 1-3 grams of weight per week as they grow.

Weaning

Although baby degus can eat solid food within a few hours of their birth, they need their mother's milk in the first weeks of their lives.

Pups should not be weaned until they are at least six weeks of age.

Placing the Pups

As tempting as it is to breed degus to have those adorable pups in the house, you have to think about the welfare of the animals first. It's likely not going to be practical for you to keep them all, so get them placed in advance.

If you don't have a plan for the babies to go to good homes where they will be well cared for, rethink the whole endeavor.

Chapter 4 – Degu Health and Breeding

Because degus have been bred in captivity to serve as lab animals, and because they are subject to genetic abnormalities, it's really best to leave breeding to professionals.

If, however, you have a pair of degus and an unplanned litter comes along, immediately begin developing a plan to make sure the babies will be adopted under the best circumstances possible.

Should you be forced to keep the pups for an extended period of time, immediately set up new quarters or expand your existing set up to make sure all the degus have adequate space for optimal health, exercise, and wellbeing.

Degu Quick Facts – Watching the Babies Grow

Like all caviomorph babies, degu pups come into the world with a lot of their abilities already in place, and their eyes open.

Day One:

The pups will be able to walk and groom, including licking their paws and washing their faces.

Day Two:

They begin to use their hind feet to scratch themselves.

Day Three:

The babies become more coordinated with their grooming, and start keeping themselves very clean.

Day Four:

The pups start to sit upright and have a good look around.

Day Five:

Look out! The babies are now figuring out how to run and jump.

Day Six:

Their grooming habits now extend to washing their belly fur.

Day Eight:

Now the little degus are spending all of their time playing.

At two weeks, the little ones are happily taking dust baths, standing up like proper degus, using a full range of vocalizations, and rough housing with their litter mates.

Degus in Brief

A brownish/gray caviomorph rodent indigenous to the western slopes of the Andes Mountains in Chile. Closely related to the chinchilla and the guinea pig. Also called: brush-tailed rat, Chilean squirrel, or trumpet-tailed rat.

Average Cost to Purchase:

$20-$40 / £13-£25 per individual
$40-$80 / £25-£50 or less per pair

Native Habitat: Semi-arid scrub brush.

Basic Behavior: Burrowing, diurnal, herbivore that is semifossorial, spending part of the day above ground foraging for food.

Average Weight: 6-10.5 ounces (170-298 grams)

Body Length: 5-8 inches (13-20 cm)

Length of Tail: 5 inches (13 cm)

As Pets: Highly agreeable. Enjoy being held on their own terms and petted. Happiest in pairs. Equally social by gender. Not recommended for interaction with other household pets. Not suitable as a pet for young children.

Activity Level: High. Love to run, jump, and climb. An exercise wheel is a must with this species.

Degus in Brief

Out-of-Cage Time: One-half hour per day minimum.

Ideal Room Temperature: 70° F / 21° C

Precautions: The tail is subject to "de-gloving," detaching from the body as an added protection against predators.

Negative Behavior: Chewing. Must have numerous chew toys.

Maintenance Level: Moderate. Fastidious, with low urine output, but highly specific housing and dietary requirements. Spot cleaning daily, thorough bedding change once a week, deep cleaning once a month.

Minimum Cage Size:

- 27.5 inches / 70 cm long
- 18 inches / 46 cm wide
- 39 inches / 99 cm high

Do NOT purchase a cage with a wire mesh floor. Degus like taller cages as opposed to those that are long.

Appropriate Substrates: Pine shaving, paper bedding, hay or straw.

Dietary Essentials: Unlimited supply of grass hay, for instance timothy. Pellet foods, either degu or chinchilla specific products. Some fresh vegetable content. Extremely limited amounts of fruit once a month.

Unsafe Pellet Foods: Mixes formulated for rabbits, hamsters, and gerbils.

Required Supplementation: Vitamin C

Grooming: Dust bath required with commercially available chinchilla dust products.

Health Facts:

Vaccinations - Not required.

Spaying and neutering - Only neutering of males recommended.

Common conditions - Dental problems (spurs, overgrown teeth), diabetes, cataracts, pododermatitis (bumblefoot), infections (abscesses, respiratory, etc.), gastrointestinal (constipation, diarrhea, and bloat), dehydration, heat stroke.

Medication Sensitivities:

- Metoclopramide
- Fusidic acid
- Trimethoprim
- Sulfamethoxazole

Tolerant of both isoflourane and ketamine anesthesia.

Generally tolerant of broad spectrum antibiotics.

Breeding Facts:

Sexually mature at 53-55 weeks.
Gestation is 90-93 days.

Average litter size is 6 pups.

Should not be weaned before six weeks of age.

Weight at birth 0.5 ounce / 14 grams.

Afterword

Even though the scientific record can't conclusively pinpoint the origin of the degu, they are so well-adapted to their native environment on the western slopes of the Chilean Andes that in some areas they number as many as 100 per acre.

Like many rodents, degus were originally seen as purely medical research animals. They have a propensity for developing both diabetes and cataracts.

If the pups are taken away from their mothers too soon, the juveniles develop ADHD-like behavior problems. Older degus develop brain lesions that are strikingly similar to those seen in Alzheimer's patients.

By the 1960s, however, the degu's sunny disposition and bright intelligence caught the attention of enthusiasts who began to keep the little rodents as companion animals.

They are undeniably cute, with bright black eyes, generous whiskers, a bushy tail, and alert ears. Most people think a degu looks like a cross between a squirrel and a rat, with more of the squirrel cuteness and all of the rat's keen intelligence.

Degus live on average 8 years, which is much longer than other companion rodents. They are wide awake during the day, fastidious in their habits, and openly affectionate after they've gotten to know their new family.

Afterword

Happiest when kept in pairs, degus are quite agreeable to same gender "roomies" with few signs of aggression or territoriality.

If you are keeping a male and female and do not want to breed the animals, it's recommended that the male be neutered rather than risk spaying the female.

Beyond these considerations, degus are low maintenance pets. They do need a great deal of room as they are active runners and jumpers, but their urine output is minimal and typically confined to one area of the cage.

Although more difficult to find than other pet rodents, a degu makes a marvelous, engaging pet. They are not recommended as pets for children without close adult supervision, but they are still a terrific addition to a household and very well suited to apartment life needing only half an hour or so a day out of their cages.

If you do decide to bring a degu into your life, be prepared to give the little creature your heart. You won't be able to help it. They're just that charming!

Relevant Websites

Degutopia
www.degutopia.co.uk

Degu Cage
www.degucage.com

Animal Diversity Web
www.animaldiversity.ummz.umich.edu/accounts/Octodon
_degus

Degu Information
www.degus.com/deguz.html

The Degu Home Page Information
www.degu.leliveld.org/index2.html

World Association of Zoos and Aquariums
www.waza.org/en/zoo/visit-the-zoo/rodents-and-
hares/octodon-degus

Degu International
www.octodondegus.weebly.com/ten-steps-to-keeping-
happier-and-healthier-degus.html

Pet Info Packets: Degu
www.petinfopackets.com/degus/deguinfopacket.html

Degu Information Page
www.degus-online.de/english.htm

Degu World
www.myhomezone.co.uk/degus

eRodent
www.erodent.co.uk/DegusIndex.htm

Don't Forget – you can join us FREE

http://www.DeguBook.com

Frequently Asked Questions

Although I recommend you read the full text to understand degu husbandry, these are some of the more frequently asked questions about these clever little animals and their behaviors.

Why would I want a degu instead of a gerbil or a guinea pig?

Degus carry the advantage of being longer lived than most other companion rodents. The average age in captivity is about 8-9 years, although some individuals have reached age 13.

Additionally, degus are active during the day, and are very clean. When handled on their own terms, the little animals are quite affectionate. They are also highly intelligent.

When I let my degu have time out of the cage, he starts to dig. Is that normal?

Yes, by nature degus are semifossorial. They spend part of their time underground in burrows, and the other portion above ground foraging for food.

Digging is a natural instinct. Some individuals are more prone to dig than others. If you want to keep them occupied and protect the floor, give them a box filled with substrate to play in outside of the cage.

What kinds of sounds do degus make?

Degus have a large vocabulary of sounds. These include "calls" like those between a mother and her pups, or those used for social contact among adults.

There are also sounds for aggression and warning. Degus also communicate with their tails, by drumming and beating.

When are degus most active?

By nature, degus are awake during the day, making them "diurnal." They are highly adaptable, however, and over time their patterns will come to mimic your own.

Why is my degu awake at night?

If you are leaving the exercise wheel in your degu's cage at all times, he may be choosing to go to the "gym" at night because it's cooler.

Try taking the wheel out of the cage and lower the temperature slightly in the room to encourage your pet to run in his wheel during the day.

What should I do to stop biting behavior in my degu?

If you've just gotten your degu, it might not be used to you yet. When degus are stressed, they will bite. It's also possible you're picking him up in a way he doesn't like.

It's better to let degus come to you rather than pick them up with a hand around the middle (which they hate) or running them into a corner.

New mothers will bite out of a desire to defend their pups. It's best not to handle the pups before they're weaned. The solution to the biting may be something as simple as washing your hands before interacting with your pet. If your fingers smell like food, your degu may think you're one big treat!

Never yell at your pet. When the degu bites, make a squeaking or yelping noise to indicate you're in pain. If the degu is really just trying to groom you, he'll understand the sound and be more gentle.

How smart are degus?

Degus have shown examples of extreme intelligence in behavioral testing, including the use of very simple tools and a capacity to sort objects by size.

They are certainly social and adaptive, and are highly observant of what goes on in their environment.

Are degus trainable?

Degus react well to training. They are not only intelligent, but affectionate with their humans, so they have an innate desire to please.

It's important to teach them to climb into your hand so you can pick them up properly without injuring their fragile tails. As startling as it sounds, a degu's tail will come right off if the animal is scared and thinks it needs to get away.

Your pet will learn its name quickly, and will respond to both hand and verbal signals. All that's really required to train a degu is patience, positive reinforcement, and a little imagination.

Should I buy more than one degu?

In their native habitat in Chile, degus live in groups, interacting through a range of social behavior. The little animals groom each other, play, and share burrows.

In captivity, a lone degu will become depressed and may even fall ill if it doesn't have enough company.
No matter how much you love your little pet, you will likely not be able to fill all its social needs. It's really best to keep multiple degus. This arrangement works quite well since same gender pairs get along superbly with no squabbling. Unless there's competition for a mate, males rarely if ever fight.

Do degus groom their humans?

Absolutely. Degus groom each other, and as they bond with you, they show their affection and trust by grooming you as well.

When you tickle your pet's belly or scratch its little ears, the degu interprets your actions as a sort of grooming, so it's all more or less a mutual admiration society!

I have two male degus. They don't seem to be fighting per se, but they do kick at each other sometimes and make noises. Should I be concerned?

Degus engage in play fighting that can look very realistic. If the two little guys are just chattering at each other, they're having fun and it's nothing to worry about.

If they were really angry, there would be a lot of grunting, and the aggression would be overt. Degus may be small, but when they fight, they mean business.

Do degus like to be held?

Degus don't like to be restrained, but when they are familiar and comfortable with a person who knows how to correctly handle them, they are very affectionate pets.

Degus do not like to be picked up with a hand around their middle. In their mind, that's equal to being captured by a predator. They will wriggle and fight to get loose, and they won't trust you after the incident.

It's best to first teach a degu to step onto your outstretched hand and then "hold" the little creature on his terms. Soon you'll have a little pet that enjoys sitting on your arms and shoulders and that is receptive to ear and tummy scratches.

When a degu is relaxed, it will sit very still and stay with you for long periods of time — even to the point of falling asleep.

Why does my degu seem to freeze in place, especially when she's first taken out of the cage and put down?

When a degu freezes in place, it's generally afraid and anxious. The little animal is trying not to be seen in case there's a hungry predator nearby.

If your pet doesn't relax after a few seconds and begin to explore, you may want to return the degu to its habitat and think of ways to make time outside the cage feel safer.

In the wild, do degus store food in their burrows?

Degus store food in two ways, in their burrows and on the surface. Degus don't hibernate the way squirrels do, but they still keep a supply of food on hand since they spend their time underground in especially hot weather.

Even captive degus will occasionally try to bury their food. It just means your little pet is full, but wants to save the treat for later.

Why does my degu roll on the floor?

Your degu is probably rolling on an area that has been scent marked. The rolling behavior is the same thing they do in their dust bath, so your pet may be asking you for more time in the sand.

It's important to give your pet lots of access to dust for rolling as this will keep its coat and skin in good shape and protect the degu from external parasites.

My degu is constantly flicking its tail. What is he "saying?"

Unless your degu is a male trying to make a date with his lady love, he's probably just excited and interested in what's going on around him.

As part of the mating ritual, male degus thump the ground with their tail. Males will also flick their tails at newcomers as a territorial warning.

Remember that all degus are individuals. The species does have a common "language," but any one degu will have forms of expression all its own. If you watch your pet closely, you'll get the message.

How can I tell if the temperature is right for my degu?

The ideal temperature for a degu is 70° F / 21° C. They come from a warm climate, and do tend to get cold, sitting hunched up with their fur fluffed out. Wild degus will sun, and then return underground when they get too warm.

You don't want to position your pet's cage in front of a window due to the danger of overheating, but don't be surprised if you see your degu seeking out a little sun puddle for a few minutes.

How can I be sure a room is safe for my degu to run around?

Refer to Chapter 2 for a full discussion of "degu proofing" a room. The real key to safety is getting all the potential hazards out of the space and making sure there are no viable escape routes.

Don't underestimate your degu. These little guys are great climbers, and when they are curious about something, they will find a way to check it out.

Be especially vigilant about wires. Degus take "test" nibbles to find out if something is edible. If that something is an electrical cable, the consequences can be deadly.

Also make sure to get all plants out of the room. They're not all toxic, but it's too hard to sort out what is and isn't. Removing all plants is the safer option.

How can I be sure I'm helping my degu keep its teeth worn down?

The best way to safeguard your degu's dental health is to make sure your pet never runs out of good quality, fresh, grass hays. Never over feed your degu pellet food. The more you encourage your degu to eat hay, the healthier its teeth will be. Don't worry. There's no such thing as "too much" hay for a degu.

(For a full discussion on degu dental health, see the sections on diet, nutrition, and health.)

Appendix 1 – List of Breeders

Benjamin's Ark
alifewithanimals.webs.com
hobby breeder
Essex, UK

Degutopia
www.degutopia.co.uk

Hoobly Classifieds
www.hoobly.com
Category Pets & Animals / Exotic Pets
Not a consistent source, but listings do appear.

Mill City Degus
Lowell, Massachusetts
978-937-7287
www.millcitydegus.com

Pet Classifieds
www.pet-classifieds.com
Not a consistent source, but listings do appear.

Pets4Homes
www.pets4homes.com

Category Rodents, Degus
Not a consistent source, but listings do appear.

Appendix 1 – List of Breeders

S & S Exotic Animal Inc.
Houston, Texas 77039
281-590-0426
www.sandsexoticanimals.com

Small Furries for Sale in United Kingdom
www.gumtree.com

www.gumtree.com/small-furries/uk/degus

Not a consistent source, but listings do appear.

Appendix 2 – Legal Information

Please note that legal regulations are subject to change. If you are in doubt about the legality of owning a degu in your state or area, contact your local wildlife authority for more information.

United States

Alabama – Illegal

Alaska – Illegal

Arizona – Permit required.

Arkansas – Must present proof of legal acquisition.

California – Illegal

Colorado – Permit may be required.

Connecticut – Permit required.

Delaware – Permit required.

District of Columbia – Legal

Florida – Legal

Georgia – Illegal

Hawaii – Illegal

Idaho – Illegal

Illinois – Legal

Indiana – Legal

Iowa - Legal

Kansas – Legal

Kentucky – May require a permit.

Louisiana – Legal

Maine – Legal

Maryland - Legal

Massachusetts – Legal

Michigan – Legal

Minnesota – Legal

Mississippi – Legal

Missouri - Legal

Montana - Legal

Nebraska - Legal

Nevada - Legal

New Hampshire – May require a permit.

New Jersey – May require a permit.

New Mexico – Legal

New York – May require a permit.

North Carolina - Legal

North Dakota – May require a permit.

Ohio – May require a permit.

Oklahoma – May require a permit.

Oregon – May require a permit.

Pennsylvania - May require a permit.

Rhode Island - Legal

South Carolina - Legal

South Dakota – Permit required.

Tennessee – May require a permit.

Texas – Legal

Utah – Illegal

Vermont – Illegal

Virginia – Illegal

Washington – Legal

West Virginia – Permit required.

Wisconsin – May require a permit.

Wyoming – Permit required.

United Kingdom

Degus are legal to own as pets throughout the United Kingdom.

Glossary

A

Agouti - The name that describes the alternating bands of light and dark coloration in the fur of a degu.

B

Bedding - Any material used in the bottom of your degu's cage is referred to as bedding. The favored material is pine.

C

Cage - Pet degus are typically kept in cages as their primary habitat. The best selection is a tall cage with few plastic parts since degus chew vigorously. The cage should include features to allow for jumping and climbing like shelves, solid ramps, and platforms.

Caviomorph - A group of rodents that includes guinea pigs, chinchillas and degus.

Chew toys - It is absolutely essential to provide your degu with safe toys for chewing. Hard wood items that do not contain dyes and that have not been exposed to insecticides and chemicals are the best choices. Avoid hard plastics as your pet may swallow the fragments. Chew toys are necessary for proper dental health.

Chuck weed – A vocalization unique to the degu described as a garbled cluck progressing to a buzzing chuckle. The sound indicates alert interest.

D

De-gloving – The defensive mechanism that allows a degu's tail to release from the animal's body to facilitate escape from a predator.

Degu proof - This is the process of making a room or an area safe for a degu to spend time out of its cage. Since degus chew so vigorously, it's important to secure all potential hazards like electrical cords, and to make sure your pet does not have access to toxic substances.

Dehydration – A potentially life-threatening lack of moisture in the tissues of the body.

Diurnal - An animal that is awake and active during the daylight hours.

Dust bath - Rather than bathing in water, degus prefer to roll in dust to clean oil and dirt out of their fur. Special dust for this purpose is available online or in pet stores.

E

Enurination – During mating, the practice exhibited by a male degu when he sprays urine over the female.

G

Gestation - The period of time that elapses between conception and birth.

I

Incisors - In degus, the incisors are the two long front teeth that are located in the center of both the top and bottom jaw.

M

Molt -The process by which an animal sheds all or a portion of its coat on a regular basis.

N

Nest box - A wooden or cardboard box in which your degu will sleep or hide. Line the nest box with pine wood shavings, but do not use cedar which is toxic.

Nocturnal - Animals that are most active at night and that sleep during the day are said to be nocturnal.

P

Pilo-erection - Refers to the ability of an animal to raise the hairs of its coat to appear larger to a potential predator.

Pododermatitis – Painful pressure sores on the feet of a companion animal such as a degu housed in a cage with a wire mesh bottom or other rough surface. Commonly known as bumblefoot.

S

Semifossorial – Animals that spend a portion of their lives below ground in burrows.

Index

Index

Index

Suggestions / Reviews

I really hope you liked the book and found it useful.

A LOT of time and hard work went into writing it. I have loved degus for years and thought it was about time I put some knowledge down on paper for others to use.

Almost certainly you purchased this book online so I'm sure you'll be contacted soon asking for your review of it by the book seller you ordered it through. I would be very, very grateful if you could provide a positive review please.

However, if you are unhappy with the book or feel I have left information out then please do get in contact first (before leaving the review) and hopefully I can help.

I'm happy to rewrite / add sections if you feel it would improve the book for other readers in the future. Simply email me at:

susan@degubook.com

with your suggestions and I'll get back to you as soon as I can (it may take a few days). If I can I will then act on your ideas and revise the book and send you a free copy (and others who joined our free club via http://www.degubook.com) with the updated book ASAP just as a 'thank you' for helping to improve it.

Thank you again

Susan Moore

Printed in Great Britain
by Amazon.co.uk, Ltd.,
Marston Gate.